31 Days of Quiet Time
Devotions for the Soul

31 Days of Quiet Time

Devotions for the Soul

Erika McCoy

IDYLLIC PUBLISHING

2020

First Printing: 2021
ISBN 978-1-7362533-1-1
Idyllic Publishing
Bowie, Maryland 20716

Dedication

To my family and dear friends—thank you for encouraging me to *just write*! Without your support, I wouldn't have gone through with publishing my first book. And sincere thanks to my editor, who cheerfully enabled me to share my innermost thoughts with the world.

Contents

31 Days of Quiet Time
Devotions for the Soul

Preface

For years, I knew that I was going to write a book. But instead of writing, all I did was ask God, "What am I to say?" My constant thought was, "There are so many other authors out there; really good ones. Surely, they've covered it all." Just like Moses, I made excuses for what God told me to do. After years of self-doubt, it finally dwelled upon me that God said to Moses in Exodus 4:11-12 that He would be with his (Moses's) mouth and guide him in what to say.

Moses had many questions for God. And God finally gave into Moses's banter, but He was angered by it. Moses's lack of faith was likely disappointing to God. I've probably angered God too by not acknowledging His calling for me in all these years. Out of fear, I was hesitant to write. I chose fear over faith, which isn't pleasing to God.

Reading Exodus reminded me today that God will be my mouthpiece. Throughout this journey, it has been a daily struggle to get over myself and just write! I don't know who God wants me to write to or in what form, but I know He has placed an undying passion in my heart to write. As you read, I hope this book blesses you in ways unimaginable—in the same way that it has blessed me as I wrote each word.

Day 1: Obedience Versus Skill

God is my strength and power, And He makes
my way perfect.
II Samuel 22:33 (NKJV)

I don't know about you, but the thought of doing things in a less than perfect way frazzles me. I'm a bit of a perfectionist, to a fault. Reading this verse reminded me to be obedient to God rather than rely on my skills. God calls us to do things in excellence, truly, but my issue is withholding work until I feel it's perfect. I tend not to start a task or goal until I think I have it all figured out. My desire for perfection applies to many areas of my life, this book being one example.

As I stated in the foreword, I believe that God has given me the gift of encouraging others through written word. I dare to call myself a writer, but I've dreamt of being one. In the meantime, I write with others in mind. Nevertheless, I've been fearful to share my writing. I don't have exact clarity on the game plan. I mentally spin out and end up producing nothing! In spite of my uncertainties, I know I must be obedient and trust that God has me covered. I need to accept in my heart that I don't need to rely on my skills. God has it all figured out!

My Prayer

Lord, please direct my path, encourage my heart, and sensitize my ears to hear Your prompting. Give me the desire to follow You even when I feel unprepared. I want to trust You, Lord, and I acknowledge that my perfectionism is a sign of fear. Forgive me for not wholeheartedly trusting You. Thank You for loving me, anyway. In Jesus's name I pray, Amen.

Day 2: Things You Don't Know

Call to Me, and I will answer you, and show you
great and mighty things, which you do not know.
Jeremiah 33:3 (NKJV)

Have you ever felt like you were repeating the same mistakes over and over again? I sometimes find myself praying over the same issues, which suggests that I'm traveling down the same pathway, with no sign of progress. When this happens, I find myself frustrated and reeling, trying to figure out what I'm doing wrong.

This verse blessed me with a new prayer and a fresh perspective. Obviously, my prayers have become just as stagnant as I feel and limited to only what I know. Is it possible that I've prevented a breakthrough from happening by praying such low-level prayers? Today, I'm demonstrating faith and hope by asking God to guide me to things that I don't know are even possible, things that are greater than I can imagine. And I'm expecting Him to do it. Will you join me in calling on Him?

My Prayer

Lord God, You're great and mighty! Forgive me for losing hope and sticking with the familiar. Lord, I call on You today. Please hear me. I pray that You'll do great and mighty things that I don't know. I don't know what I don't know, but You do. Change my perspective, my heart, and my sight to see and feel what You're doing. I don't want to miss it! Thank You, Father, for Your love, grace, and mercy. Bless those saying this prayer. Transform us. I pray and give thanks in Jesus's name. Amen.

Day 3: You Aren't the Only One

Keep a cool head. Stay alert. The Devil is poised to pounce, and would like nothing better than to catch you napping. Keep your guard up. You're not the only ones plunged into these hard times. It's the same with Christians all over the world.
1 Peter 5:9-11 (MSG)

Tough times—you've probably been through one or are currently going through one. In those difficult moments, it feels like no one else could possibly understand what you're going through. This Scripture reminds us that other Christians (all over the world, mind you) are also experiencing challenges. The enemy can be so crafty. During those moments of emotional weakness, you may be inclined to drop your faith guard. The enemy will then try to convince you that no one else understands your situation. As a natural response, you turn inward and isolate yourself from others.

Next thing that might happen is that you stop talking to those who are able to give you the Lord's perspective, people who could pray for you and help change your mindset about whatever it is you're going through. However, the enemy has whispered a lie, "Those folks can't understand. Keep it to yourself. You can figure it out on your own." You then stop answering calls, emails, or texts from your friends. As cycles work, their natural response may be to stop reaching out to you and give you the space that they think you're silently requesting. Then the enemy will say, "I told you, they don't care about you." All lies. Meanwhile, you've bought into the initial lie that you're the only one going through whatever you're going through. It's a cycle of lies, all orchestrated by the enemy, to steal your faith.

When you find yourself in tough times, pray for your faith to be strengthened; that you may be surrounded by others who are able to empathize with you and give you proper perspective on your situation. And most of all, pray that you'll not fall prey to the lies of the enemy.

My Prayer

Lord God, thank You for Your Word, which reminds me that I'm never alone. You haven't forgotten about me nor forsaken me. When we fall into trials, they're only for a season. Remind me that my trials won't last forever. Other Christians are going through trials as well, and they can empathize with us. Ultimately, You understand us best, and if we don't have anyone who can listen and give us a better perspective, You're always waiting to hear from us. You'll always hear our prayers, and I pray that we have sensitive ears and hearts to hear Your response. I love You, Lord. I pray that the person reading this message today, who is losing hope, feels Your power and love. Send an encouraging word their way to remind them that You're greater than their situation. Thank You, Lord, for Your grace and mercy. Amen.

Day 4: I Am With You

> Do not fear [anything], for I am with you; Do not
> be afraid, for I am your God. I will strengthen you,
> be assured I will help you; I will certainly take
> hold of you with My righteous right hand [a hand
> of justice, of power, of victory, of salvation].
> Isaiah 41:10 (AMP)

Just when I started worrying about making a decision and wondered if the Lord was going to be with me, I read this verse. This verse is a reminder that He is always with me. Fear has a crazy grip on me from time to time. But this verse settles my mind battle. The winning statement is, "What's to fear if the Lord is with me?" Isaiah 41:10 reminds us that when troubles come, the Lord is right there. Basically, no matter what we're facing, He is there. Why is that so hard to remember when we're in the midst of 'drama'?

As I've matured as a Christian, I've gotten better at calling out to the Lord first when I'm faced with a challenge. But I still revert back to old habits from time to time, like picking up the phone and calling everyone, except the Lord, to discuss my issues. This verse reminds me that the Lord, and only the Lord, can strengthen me.

My Prayer

Lord, thank You for Your greatness. Even when I forget about You, You never forget about me. I know this because Your Word says so. I know that life won't always go the way I want, and disappointments will occur. But I trust that You'll strengthen me just like You promised. Please remind us to come to You and patiently wait for a response. Let us not give way to fear, but let faith prevail. Amen.

Day 5: Seeking Direction

Direct my steps by Your word, And let no iniquity
have dominion over me.
Psalms 119:133 (NKJV)

Do you struggle with figuring out if you should go left or right? Making a decision is more complicated when both options seem good. How do we know which option aligns best with God's will? That's my struggle. When one of the options is overtly bad, then it's less of a decision and more of a choice to do right or wrong, which, by the way, can also be difficult. It's basically like telling your flesh to shut up! But this chapter is about the times when two seemingly good options are before you. Could one be better than the other? How are you to know?

This Scripture is the flashlight that points us back to God's Word, asking (and in my case, begging) for nothing to get in the way of hearing and following what we hear from God. This is critical. I'm certain that our "pros and cons" list is mixed with our own desires and some form of iniquity. I pray that my desires, fears, and any other ungodliness are removed so that I can hear directly (and with confidence) from God whether I'm to turn left or right.

My Prayer

Lord, please hear us. You know what we need versus what we want. You also know what is best for us. I pray that we hear from You and only You. Point us to Your Word, and silence the voices that may be misleading us. Thank You, Lord, for loving us enough to want the best for us. Open our hearts to accept Your best. Amen.

Day 6: Accepting God's Free Gifts

> Now we have received, not the spirit of the
> world, but the Spirit who is from God, that we
> might know the things that have been freely given
> to us by God.
> 1 Corinthians 2:12 (NKJV)

Why is it that we sometimes, in our human ways, want what we don't have or what the world says that we should want—fame, status, and money? Yet the very thing(s) or gifts that God has freely given us are the things that we fail to accept.

In my life, this verse plays out in how I choose to use my God-given gifts. For example, while I'm very passionate about serving students of color to ensure they receive quality education, I've struggled with how to use this social justice passion. I do feel that I have a gift of encouragement and leadership. But the issue I struggle with is how to apply my gifts appropriately. For years, I've frustratingly tried to figure this out. Thankfully, in my stumbles, I've been afforded great opportunities along the way. To be honest, I'm not clear if I'm exercising my free will by chasing after opportunities. I've had lots of challenges along the way to the point that I leave one opportunity for another. And guess what? I end up finding out that the new venture has challenges too!

The problem is that I don't make an effort to seek the Lord about what He has freely given me and then accept it. This free gift could certainly be interpreted as salvation, which I've graciously accepted. But what I'm speaking of are the free gifts that we all have been given by the Holy Spirit to do God's good work. Once we accept those gifts and walk in them, then true peace and freedom are waiting for us. I've frequently tried to conjure what I think is the right path, when oftentimes the very gift that I withhold from sharing with others is the one He is waiting for me to accept and use!

From this point onwards, there shall be no more questioning if this is the right or wrong choice, but rather a solid knowledge that it's right, even when it doesn't feel good. There's something freeing about knowing that you're doing exactly what the Lord has given you the gifts to do for those He has called you to share them with. Sometimes it may not look as you expected, but all it takes is accepting God's gifts, which are free from Him and ultimately will be freeing for you.

My Prayer

Lord God, please forgive me for my unwillingness to accept Your free gifts. I fight with You about what and who You're calling me to be. In some situations, I just don't know. But I'm reminded to be obedient in the small things, because my choices of today set up the path for tomorrow.* Please give me a sensitive heart and spirit to hear You and the willingness to follow, despite what my flesh wants or what the world says. Thank You, Lord, for the freedom waiting for me on the other side of the door marked "Obedience." Amen.

Additional Scriptures to meditate: Ephesians 4:7-8 NKJV—But to each one of us grace was given according to the measure of Christ's gift. Therefore, He says: "When He ascended on high, He led captivity captive, And gave gifts to men."

*Rephrase of Lysa Terkeurst's *The Best Yes*.

Day 7: Do You Feel Forgotten?

> I am forgotten like a dead man, out of mind; I am
> like a broken vessel. But as for me, I trust in You,
> O Lord; I say, "You are my God."
> Psalms 31:12, 14 (NKJV)

There are times when it seems as if I've been forgotten about by family, friends, and sometimes even God. I hesitate to add "by God **too**" because deep down, I know it isn't true. But in the many moments when everyone else seems to be doing their own thing, I do fall into the self-pity dialogue, "What about me?" In anger, when I feel like I'm pouring out and really doing my best, only to get a half-hearted thank you, or even worse, no acknowledgement at all, my inner dialogue sounds more like, "Lord, have You forgotten about me?"

Of course not! He hasn't forgotten about me. And if you're like me, wondering the same thing from time to time—no, He hasn't forgotten about you. Maybe your marriage has been in a rut; things seem like they'll never change for the better. Or perhaps you work hard at your job, but you've never been promoted or acknowledged. Another example is that you passionately serve others, but they show little appreciation for your dedication. I'm happy to share this with you—you can stop being concerned about whether others have forgotten about you, because it doesn't matter. Do unto the Lord...He hasn't forgotten, but He needs our focus on Him, not on them! When I start that tired, self-pitying dialogue, I have to bring myself back, because I'm shifting my focus from God to them. And even worse is when I'm focusing solely on me (and I mean that in a selfish sort of way). During times of discouragement, I want to be like the Psalmist and be able to say with conviction, "I trust You, Lord!"

My Prayer

Lord, please forgive me for my self-centered ways. I get down and out sometimes when I feel like I'm doing what I should be doing but I'm not being rewarded. Please change my motivation, my mindset, and ultimately my heart. Lord, give me Your perspective. Help me to work, serve, and love others as unto You. Humble me, Lord. Remove the prideful spirit that rises up when I want to be put first. Thank You for loving me anyway. I trust You, and I love You, Lord. Please save and capture the heart of the reader who doesn't feel the same for You. May they come to know You as their personal Savior. Amen.

> But those who wait on the Lord Shall renew their strength; They shall mount up with wings like eagles, They shall run and not be weary, They shall walk and not faint.
> Isaiah 40:31 (NKJV)

Why does the word "wait" seem like one of the worst words created? Actually, the word "patience" is also running the race for first place with "wait." And that's right, it takes patience to wait, especially for something you really want (or think you want). This might not pertain to you, but I know this is an area of growth for me and one that I try to consider when I become frustrated.

If I can just slow down, grow in patience (while not becoming complacent) and, for heaven's sake, not get weary! That's a tall order, but thank goodness that we have the Lord's strength to rely upon. Likely (or definitely, in fact), the reason why I struggle in this area is because instead of relying on the Lord, I'm relying on me, myself, and I. What about you—why are you struggling to wait?

My Prayer

Lord, thank You for Your strength! I'm filled with awe when I try to conceive how You have enough strength for everyone and that You think enough of me to give it to me when I need it. Please forgive me for all the times that I've tried to take things into my own hands instead of laying it on the altar and allowing You to do what You promised to do. Forgive me, Lord, for running ahead at times and not patiently waiting for the green light from You. I thank You that You love me enough to rein me back in and give me another chance to wait on You, time and time again. You're so awesome, and I pray that the reader is inspired to trust You and wait for Your direction. And when they do act upon Your guidance, I pray that they don't grow weary in doing Your work. In Jesus's name, Amen.

Fear not, for I am with you; Be not dismayed, for I am your God. I will strengthen you, Yes, I will help you, I will uphold you with My righteous right hand.
Isaiah 41:10 (NKJV)

If you've ever experienced fear, whether it's fear of rejection or fear of a situation or person, this verse is for you! Fear is debilitating; it stops you from doing what God has called you to do and prevents you from being who God has called you to be. As I look toward the future, I've made up my mind to reject fear.

While I'm aware that this Scripture was written at a time when physical wars and enemies were at hand, it reminds me of my own "war"—the war that takes place in my mind. My enemy can sometimes be my own thoughts. So whenever I sense that fear is at the root of a decision or when I begin to avoid a situation out of fear, this verse becomes my mantra. I'm probably not the only one who allows fear to rob me of God's goodness, but I've decided that won't be my story any longer.

My Prayer

Lord God, thank You for Your Word, love, and saving grace. I pray for each and every person gripped by fear, whatever the reason, that this reading liberates them. Lord, I pray that You open blinded eyes and closed hearts to help us see that fear isn't of You, but of the enemy of our soul. It's a tool the enemy uses to keep us bound and short of the goodness that You have for us. Lord, let this prayer bring the reader freedom to share gifts with others. I pray that fear of rejection will no longer hold them back. For those who've been fearful to give their hearts to You, may this reading inspire them, serving as a reminder that You have us safe within Your loving hands. Thank You, Lord. In Your Son's name, Amen.

Day 10: Freedom from Stinking Thinking

Trust in the Lord with all your heart, And lean
not on your own understanding; In all your ways
acknowledge Him, And He shall direct your
paths.
Proverbs 3:5-6 (NKJV)

This verse is a constant reminder for me to break away from my stinking thinking! I get caught up in so many thoughts sometimes, to the point that I can't follow the conversations happening in my own head (I know that sounds crazy!). But with some maturity and growth in Christ, I'm now able to notice when my mood is off and question myself. Nine out of ten times, the issue is that I've attempted to solve some issue in my head. Mixed into those thoughts, the enemy inevitably drops a "stinkin thinkin" seed that I'm inadequate or unskilled, which leads me to ACTUALLY believe that. Then my entire mood shifts. "Wait," whispers my spirit during this internal dialogue. And my spirit asks me, "Are you leaning to your own understanding **again**?"

Trying to figure things out based upon your own understanding causes you to consider yourself inadequate! IF you would just STOP trying to figure everything out and pray about your dilemma, then the Lord will direct your path. And by pray, I don't mean continuing to voice **your** plans to the Lord, but confess your sins of anxiety and the attempt to be the lord of your life, then put your concerns on His mighty altar. Ask for direction. Ask for your ears to be open, your heart to be willing, and your mind to be QUIET!

So if you're like me and have experienced a battle of the mind, this Scripture is a must know! It can help you get the release from the hold the enemy wants to have on you. He wants to keep you entrenched in all those thoughts so that he can drop his "stinkin" seeds, which might go unchallenged because there are a million other thoughts happening at the same time. Check those thoughts as soon as they start to overwhelm you...that's a trigger that you're leaning on your own understanding! Quiet yourself immediately and PRAY!

My Prayer

Lord God, thank You for Your love and new mercies granted to us each morning! Please forgive us for leaning on our own understanding. We know Your greatness, but we get caught in our flesh and pridefulness; forgive us. Lord, we confess our need for You in every crevice of our lives. Direct our paths and give us peace about whatever direction You set for us. Let us know that it's You speaking by the peace we'll have. Quiet our minds, sensitize our ears, and encourage our hearts so that we obediently follow You. We love You, Lord. In Jesus's name, Amen.

Day 11: Patience and Hope

Feeling hopeless? You're not alone. There have been situations that I've felt hopeless about. After dealing with a trial for a long period of time or certain people who don't seem to change, yes, I start to lose hope. Reading this Scripture has taught me that I'm to:

- Learn from the Scriptures—got it! For why else would I keep reading the Bible?
- Have hope—got it! We find the promises of God and words of encouragement in stories throughout the Scriptures.
- Have patience with the Scriptures—I had to re-read that part over and over.

Then it clicked! In fact, it made me cringe. The lesson from this Scripture is that I'm to have:

- Patience regarding what God says He'll do.
- Patience regarding what God wants to do in me.
- Patience that the Truth (i.e., His Word) and my circumstances will come into alignment one day (just not according to my timetable), hence the deliberately placed two-syllable word beginning with "P"—patience.

So today's lesson (for me) is that hope is birthed out of PATIENCE. God's Word is full of comfort and hope meant not only for others, but also for me. Hope is a choice. I can choose impatience, ultimately leading to a feeling of hopelessness. Or I can choose to be patient and have hope and comfort in God's Word, which says that as long as I pray according to His will, He hears me. I have the confidence (and hope) that my prayers will come to fruition.*

My Prayer

Why, Lord, do I struggle to believe You, especially when things around me don't feel good? I struggle with the need for harmony and comfort; nowhere does Your Word promise that I'll always have both. I thank You for Your constant love; for sending words of comfort and for pricking our spirits to help us be more like You. Thank You, Lord, for Your Word and Your Son, who allows me to live life and live it more abundantly. In Jesus's name I pray, Amen.

*Rephrase of 1 John 5:14-15.

Day 12: Proud to Be Me

Many times in my life, I've compared myself to others, wishing that I looked like them, spoke like them, or had more confidence like them and so on. This verse is a reminder that God made us just the way we are, and we should be proud of that! But it doesn't mean that He won't "beat" some undesirable traits out that get in the way of bearing the fruit He intends for us.

In other situations, we "become" or behave how others want us to, out of fear of rejection. Again, the release from that stronghold (and lie from the enemy) is found in this Scripture. When you begin worrying about how others perceive you and contemplate changing who you are to appease them, read the Scripture of the day out loud to yourself as a reminder. Then say today's prayer.

My Prayer

God, thank You for fearfully and wonderfully making me. Forgive me for taking that for granted. I'm one of Your works, which makes me marvelous! I praise You for loving me enough to protect me in my mother's womb. You knew me then and created me just as You desired me to be. Lord, help me to become who You've created me to be. Release me from obsession with acceptance or the need to please others, fear of failure or rejection, or any other stronghold that keeps me from fully being who You formed me to be. I love You, Lord. Thank You for loving me. Amen.

Day 13: Stuck in the Mud

He brought me up out of the pit of destruction,
out of the miry clay, And He set my feet upon a
rock making my footsteps firm.
Psalm 40:2 (NASB)

Are you familiar with that feeling of being stuck or slowly sinking? I can say that I have, thankfully, never been literally stuck in mud before. From what I've seen in movies, it doesn't look comfortable and can be downright scary. In my life, this feeling of "stuckness" generally occurs after I've made a big decision. I find myself regretting the decision for one reason or another; usually because my expectation wasn't fulfilled. Then I become disappointed. Unfortunately, this is a recurring pattern.

You may read this and cynically say, "Well, just make better decisions!" If that's the case, then this devotion may not be for you. On the other hand, if you've had a pattern of decisions followed by disappointment or another pattern or situation that begins to feel oh too familiar, then I think you can relate to the feeling of "stuckness." Perhaps it's not a pattern, but it's about feeling like you've been in the same situation for longer than you had hoped. Then you too might feel like you're stuck, and this devotion may speak to you.

Even though this Scripture is referring to the fact that we live in a "pit" prior to being saved, I can also see how it applies to being stuck in a situation after salvation. It can feel like you're slipping and simply can't get a grip on the situation. This Scripture reminds us that God will give us a firm place to put our feet. If we ask Him in faith and thank Him in advance, then our feet (also defined as faith and hope) will be set on firm ground. Be aware that the firm ground doesn't mean things will go your way; it means that you won't feel that overwhelming feeling of being stuck in the mud, but your burden, whatever it is, will all of a sudden seem lighter. You'll experience a sense of freedom and leave the doubting spirit down in the pit! Circumstances may not change, but your attitude toward them can and will. And when your heart is changed, your mindset shifts. Somehow, everything will seem to be alright.

Let's shift our focus today from being in the stuck place to being assured that God has our best interests at heart and that He has set our feet on solid ground. Even if your feelings don't immediately change, meditate on Psalm 40:2 and pray this prayer (or one of your own) until your heart has been changed.

My Prayer

Thank You, Lord, for making my footsteps firm. I know that if I ask for anything that's according to Your will and I ask in faith, You'll hear me. I seek You to keep me out of the miry clay. I know that I'm only stuck because I either ventured out on my own or haven't sought You in prayer and confession to place my feet on solid ground. It's so amazing that You love me enough to redeem me even when I've forsaken You. Thank You, Lord, for Your love, grace, and mercy. For those who've been suffering even while following Your will, please comfort them today. Give them the blessed assurance that they're loved and not stuck in the mud, even though it might feel that way. In Jesus's precious name I pray, Amen.

Day 14: Our Mindset—It's a Choice

> For as you know him better, he will give you,
> through his great power, everything you need for
> living a truly good life: he even shares his own
> glory and his own goodness with us! And by that
> same mighty power he has given us all the other
> rich and wonderful blessings he promised...
> 2 Peter 1:3-4(a) (TLB)

Over the years, I've learned that life is all about choices. While some events, both good and bad, are divine (meaning they're unrelated to the choices we've made), the rest of life and our worldview (how we see things) seem to be based on the choices we make. I'm not trying to freak you out or have you second guess everything you do. My hope is that this knowledge will empower you and give you a fresh perspective.

I remember a time when I persistently felt powerless and joyless. Then one day, the Glory of God was cast upon me, and He freed me from bondage. It was the bondage of feeling like I was merely existing and not really living, hoping for a better tomorrow and lamenting over what I didn't do yesterday. I was choosing to live defeated, sad, and certainly without joy. While reading these Scriptures, I learned that God has already given me what I need to live a good life. That's powerful and something truly to be joyful about! But why then did I feel so joyless and powerless before? There's only one answer—it was **my choice** to feel that way.

I'm not denying that there are people with a psychological or clinical condition that causes them to feel constantly depressed. However, for those of us who constantly feel sad in the absence of a clinical condition, believe it or not, it's a choice. We can choose to focus on the bad things happening around us instead of searching for the good. We can choose to pick out the worst in others or find the good qualities and focus upon those. We can choose to complain, even if it's silently, about our situation, or we can be grateful about what we have. I'm not asking you to look at life through rose-colored glasses. I'm aware that life is rough and really bad things happen. But we have to choose how our thoughts direct our hearts.

Will we choose to spend time on negative thoughts, which can only lead to negative emotions? Or will we process and pray about the negative thoughts, asking for a positive perspective and choosing to redirect our minds to the good instead of the bad? These verses are a reminder that we've been given God's power. It's up to us to choose to continue to develop our faith and get to know Him better. This requires maintaining a hopeful perspective. While it doesn't happen overnight, it's important for us to take control of the way we think and embrace the power we have over our thoughts.

Let today be a day that you try on the power of choices, especially regarding your thoughts and how they can monumentally shift your perspective on life. You have the power to choose joy and hope—so use it!

My Prayer

Lord, thank You for giving us Your power. Please forgive us for choosing not to use it or for using it against Your will. I pray today for those who feel hopeless, powerless, or joyless, that this devotion and Your powerful Word will ignite a new sense of energy within them. Let each reader be empowered in a new way today. Let us be reminded that You've granted us everything we need to be successful in this life. Beginning right now, let us choose love over hate, gratefulness over complaining, and empathy over judgment! Change our hearts; renew our minds and remind us that joy is a fruit of the spirit, which we received upon salvation. Thank You, Lord, for Your unending love, grace, mercy, and forgiveness. In Jesus's name I pray and give You thanks. Amen.

Day 15: Discouragement is a Choice

> For I know the thoughts that I think toward you,
> says the Lord, thoughts of peace and not of evil,
> to give you a future and a hope.
> Jeremiah 29:11 (NKJV)

The Study Bible has a lot to say about this verse, which has helped me to continue to ponder on yesterday's devotion. This could really be a duplicate message, but in really praying and studying, I would consider today's message to have a slightly different perspective about choices. One addition to yesterday's message is to note that Satan's goal is to keep us discouraged. Let's think about how that not only affects our mindset, but also our faith.

If the enemy can succeed in getting us to stay stuck in disappointment, leading to fear and self-pity, then we soon become discouraged and thus take hold of the lie that God doesn't really have good thoughts towards us. We begin to believe that God has nothing more for us than our current circumstances, especially if they're not good. Ultimately, we begin to doubt God because we're no longer believing His Word. This is a win for the enemy! He has captured our faith in God, which is all that he is after to begin with.

To counteract the enemy's attempt to destroy our faith, we have to quickly acknowledge when we've chosen to feel defeated or discouraged. It's normal to feel frustrated or sad when things aren't going according to plan or when tragedy strikes. The important thing when we experience trials isn't to allow our minds and hearts to sink into despair, which leads to discouragement. We must stay in prayer and fully confess if and when we start to doubt God. During your season of trials or tribulations, ask Him to remind you that disappointments happen, but discouragement is a choice. And if your prayer seems to go unanswered, do this simple thing—read and re-read Jeremiah 29:11 until your heart believes it.

My Prayer

Lord, thank You for having thoughts of peace and not evil toward us. Please forgive us for sometimes accepting the enemy's lies, which are intended to create doubt in our hearts about You and Your promises. Forgive us, Lord, for falling into the temptation of discouragement. Encourage our hearts and minds today, and give hope especially to those who've lost hope in You. I pray, Lord, for those who are considering suicide, that You whisper loving thoughts of encouragement to them. According to Jeremiah 29:11, remind us that Your promise is to give us a future and a hope. You've placed us all here on this earth with a specific purpose that no one can take away if we would just believe! I take hold of this promise right now and pray that others do the same. Lord, thank You for Your love. In Jesus's name I pray, Amen.

> If any of you lacks wisdom, let him ask of God,
> who gives to all liberally and without reproach,
> and it will be given to him. But let him ask in faith,
> with no doubting, for he who doubts is like a
> wave of the sea driven and tossed by the wind.
> James 1:5-6 (NKJV)

"Wait, if I need wisdom, all I have to do is just ask God!" That was the alarming thought that came to my mind after reading and re-reading these verses. But there's a catch...I have to ask for the wisdom in faith, which I honestly could use a little more of! And that leads me to the real point of this message. Why is it so hard to have faith in the first place? We place our trust in a lot of things—our cars, bank accounts, jobs, friends, spouses (hopefully) and so on! While you may say, "I don't put trust in things", please tell me how you would respond if you bought a brand new car today and it broke down on the way home. Right! You would have a fit! Why? Because you trusted that its newness equates the absence of issues.

But are trust and faith really the same? Some may argue that they're not. However, we can all agree that they certainly are related. It takes trust to have faith, meaning that if I don't have faith, or if it wavers, then I may need to check my heart and ask myself if I'm truly trusting God's Word. Even though I have the head knowledge, there are times when the heart knowledge is lacking, which is evident by my actions (or inactions).

I don't know what you desire, but I'm seeking to grow in my faith so that I can liberally ask the Lord for wisdom, because goodness knows I need it to be successful at this thing called life! When I'm feeling lost and confused, I must check my heart and ask myself if I really trust the Lord. If faith is my issue, then I need to assess how much time I'm spending with Him and reflect on all He has already done for me. His credit with me is good; I just need to remind myself of that from time to time!

My Prayer

Lord, I come to You the best way I know how. You're perfect in all Your ways; thank You for loving me in spite of my wavering faith. Lord, I ask that You increase my faith where I'm doubting You. And for the person reading this, please do the same for them. Lord God, if anyone reading this is in need of wisdom, I pray that You grant it to them so that they can make a decision that lines up with Your Word and divine purpose for their life. Thank You in advance for the confusion that You'll bind and the freedom of clarity that You'll grant someone today. You're awesome, and I thank You for hearing this prayer. In Jesus's name I pray, Amen.

Day 17: His Grace Abounds

The Law came in so that the transgression
would increase; but where sin increased, grace
abounded all the more.
Romans 5:20 (NASB)

I'm in awe of how awesome the Lord really is. No one has to remind me or convince me; I just know it. Nothing bad or good has to happen. This morning was one of those times. It happened while I was reading the Scripture for today. A sense of gratefulness overcame me! Our Lord has our best interests at heart. Of course, there are other Scriptures that directly tell us this, such as Jeremiah 29:11; so there really should be no question about that fact. Nonetheless, when I read this Scripture, it says a lot with such few words. Let's dig into it for better understanding.

Today's Scripture begins with "The Law," which refers to all of the laws introduced during the Old Testament (Mosaic laws). While laws are generally brought into existence to establish order, we can infer that these particular laws were created to justify sins. People could now defend their actions, claiming it was "according to the law." The evidence of this is outlined in the many teachings of Christ in the Gospels, especially when the Pharisees challenged Him over and over again, attempting to get Him to say something in opposition to the law.

But God! Even though sins increased, God's grace increased as well! What a great thing to know. Yet this doesn't give us a license to go sin or do more wrong. According to this Scripture, the law somewhat blinded people by preventing them from knowing that they were doing wrong. That being said, God protects us from what we don't know. He really wants us to be in His will. He's not an "I gotcha" God; His ways aren't designed to enslave or trap us. If that were the case, then He wouldn't make provisions for OUR wrongs. For that, I sit in thanks today that He has bestowed grace upon me so that when I sin and don't even know it, He doesn't brood over it and put tally marks on my "sin chart." He forgives me!

Although God doesn't hesitate to forgive our sins, as Christians, we do have a responsibility. We're to ask God to search our hearts and show us where we've sinned against Him. If we want to increase our faith and grow in our relationship with Him, we can't contently remain in an ignorant place forever. I have to willingly seek knowledge about Him and learn how my ways aren't aligned with His. He wants our hearts, and I want more of Him! Let's thank Him for His grace and also humbly ask Him to show us where we're blindly sinning against Him in our lives.

My Prayer

Thank You, Lord, for Your awesome ways. You're kind to us and incredibly loving toward us. Thank You for allowing Your grace to abound! I know that I've sinned against You in ways that I wasn't even aware of. Thank You for protecting me and for later showing me the error of my ways. I pray that the reader of this message is blessed by this Scripture and prompted to ask You to show them the error of their ways, humbly seeking Your forgiveness. I know that You have our best interests at heart, and I pray that any reader of this message, who struggles to believe that, is encouraged and reminded that You love us. Please help us to fervently seek You and humbly serve You. Thank You for Your Word, which shines a bright light on our sins if we use it to measure ourselves. In Jesus's name I pray and give You thanks, Amen.

Day 18: The Recipe for Joy

> As the Father loved Me, I also have loved you; abide in My love. If you keep My commandments, you will abide in My love, just as I have kept My Father's commandments and abide in His love. These things I have spoken to you, that My joy may remain in you, and that your joy may be full.
> John 15:9-11 (NKJV)

Searching for joy, "Joy...joy...come out, wherever you are!," is the hide-and-go-seek game that I sometimes play when I know that I'm down and out, wondering why I'm lacking joy. Sometimes it's obvious—like when a specific circumstance occurs and I can point out the issue. But there are other times when I'm just in a slump and can't explain why. In both situations, I allowed the circumstance to dictate how I feel. Over time, I've associated circumstances with happiness, which couldn't be further from the truth.

Jesus outlines very clearly in this Scripture what we need to do to have joy. It's a simple equation.

Joy (Remaining in Christ) = Doing things His way + Knowing His Word + Locking His Word into our hearts

Let's discuss parts of this equation. The Scripture says we're to "abide," meaning to remain in Christ. How gracious is Jesus in that He clarifies right away how we're to remain in Him. We have to keep His commandments. In this context, "keep" means to follow or to hold on to. This means we also have to know His Word. He ends this Scripture by encouraging us with a simple truth. But I said simple, not easy! The truth is that if we do things according to His Word (abide), then we'll have joy.

In thinking about the fact that He promises joy if I would just do things according to His Word, then the opposite is true. If I'm lacking joy, perhaps it's because I'm not keeping His Word. This gives me a serious think-about when I'm running around searching for joy. What a silly game, because joy is standing right in my face, waiting for me to simply do what God wants me to do or stop doing. My joy is directly connected to obedience of God's Word. Am I loving others the way that I should? Am I stuck in a complaining mode (i.e., I'm choosing ungratefulness, which could lead to bitterness)? Am I trying to please others or am I putting something else above God in my life (this is idolatry and a sin)? The list could go on and on. The point is this—if you and I are lacking joy, the reason shouldn't be a mystery. This Scripture clearly tells us how to have joy. So if joy is hiding in your life, check your heart, clear your mind, and pray this prayer:

My Prayer

Lord, thank You for your unending love for us. Thank You for Your Word. I pray right now that every reader is drawn to You; that their heart cries out to You, wanting more of You. Let us have the desire to do Your will. Where we're lacking joy, show us our hearts and help us to see the areas where we're not abiding in You. Let us not become depressed or guilty about our shortcomings, but may we humbly seek Your forgiveness. Give us what we need to overcome the sins we have fallen prey, and remove the strongholds that may exist in our lives. Let us have joy; let us experience the sweet taste of that inner peace and joy that only You can provide. We love You, Lord, and we thank You in advance for the shackles that'll be broken as a result of this prayer. In Jesus's name, Amen.

Day 19: Stir Up Your Gift

Therefore I remind you to stir up the gift of God
which is in you through the laying on of my
hands. For God has not given us a spirit of fear,
but of power and of love and of a sound mind.
2 Timothy 1:6-7 (NKJV)

Ever found yourself feeling afraid? Perhaps the fear isn't obvious or you aren't conscious of it. If you've found yourself feeling anxious about something and you avoid doing it, then you've possibly tried to overcome fear. For me, fear has been one of my biggest enemies! It has caused me to avoid what I know I should do, and over time, it became a lifestyle of timidity. Maybe you have a burning passion to write, start a business, or pitch a new idea at work. You shouldn't allow fear to stop you. I'm not telling you to bulldoze your way forward and abruptly quit your job to fulfill your dreams of starting a business. That wouldn't be smart. But what this message is intended to do is encourage you to deeply consider why you're avoiding that burning passion. And if fear is your enemy, then let's deal with it today—right now!

This Scripture gives us all we need to overcome fear. Even though the message was written to Timothy, it certainly applies to any believer. We're being instructed to "stir up" our gifts. I found the term "stir" to be an interesting choice of word, and upon further study, I learned that the stirring described here is like when you stir up embers (or fan a flame). Unlike stirring sugar into coffee, which is intended to blend the ingredients, this stirring is an agitation meant to ignite, such as what happens when a fire is stirred. If you fan a flame, it erupts, even when there's only a small ember left burning. On the other hand, if you don't stir or fan the embers, then the flame will die and, eventually, the fire goes out. This is exactly what we're being instructed to guard against. If we don't use our gifts, they'll decay. So the first step in overcoming fear is to begin using your gifts. If you've been hiding them or not sharing them with others, then you may as well say that you haven't been using them. Start today by identifying what gift(s) you've allowed to wither and begin using them.

The second verse (7) is a reminder that we haven't been given a spirit of fear. I found it very interesting that it follows RIGHT AFTER the instruction to use our gifts. This makes perfect sense because as human beings, once we're given direction by God (whether in the form of an idea, dream, or a deep down "knowing"), we generally need to rationalize it. Once we begin putting our logic to it, we can quickly drift into a fearful place. The fearful place sounds like, "What will people think?" or "What if the idea fails?" And if we aren't careful, we stay there—stuck in fear, doubting that we have what it takes to do whatever God has given us the passion or direction to do. We allow feelings of inadequacy to settle in and, before you know it, months or years will drift by. You'll then realize that you haven't acted upon the direction God has given you. I know this narrative too well. I've allowed logic and fear to settle in my mind far too many times. But God told us right in this Scripture that He has given us a spirit of power (courage) and a sound mind to do what He has called us to do.

So what then are you to do if fear has settled into your heart? You confess to God that you have acted like the servant man in Matthew 25:25—he was given a talent, but he buried it instead of using it. Then you begin doing whatever it is that God has instructed you to do. Lastly, put on the courage He has given you, and be prepared to experience a quieted mind, meaning that the unsettled, anxious mind that prevailed before will be quiet and joyous. Don't think that this direction has to be something big. God gives us small assignments that we ignore all the time. If you feel that you don't have direction, go back to the last thing God told you to do, and seek Him about it.

My Prayer

Lord, thank You for Your Word. You give us Your Word to convict and encourage us. The hope that lives within Your Word further demonstrates the love You have toward us—thank You! Lord God, I pray the reader of today's message confesses and renounces the spirit of fear that has choked out Your direction for their life. You've given us the ability to live abundantly, and right now, I ask for Your forgiveness where we've allowed fear to keep us beneath Your best. I pray that You reignite the passion within us if the flame has died. Lord, if Your direction has been muted by fear and inaction, then I pray that each of us will take up our gifts and begin using them today. I pray that fear has no place in our hearts and that when we feel anxious, rather than quit, that we seek You, renounce fear, and accept the power You've placed in us. Let us not try to pave our own path, but rather stay humbly directed by You. Thank You, Lord, for Your direction and forgiveness. I celebrate the yokes that'll be broken, the businesses that'll emerge, and the people that'll be touched because the readers of this message will begin stirring up the gifts that they've had all along. In Jesus's name I pray, Amen.

Day 20: Faith is an Action

> [1] Now faith is the substance of things hoped for, the evidence of things not seen.
> [7] By faith Noah, being divinely warned of things not yet seen, moved with godly fear, prepared an ark for the saving of his household, by which he condemned the world and became heir of the righteousness which is according to faith.
> Hebrews 11:1, 7 (NKJV)

The power of faith is seen throughout the entire Scriptures, but a great summary of how faith plays a role in the lives of others is probably best seen in Hebrews 11. After reading through the entire chapter, I was in awe of how the many men and women of God had displayed faith in their actions. I began to see how much I struggle in this area. In my mind, I'm a woman of faith. But when I dig a little deeper, I have to ask myself if my thoughts and actions really demonstrate the type of faith described in this Scripture.

Hebrews 11 takes an account of how Noah, Moses, Sarah, Abraham, Abel, Enoch, and many others demonstrated faith. When you look at the types of words used to describe their faith, you stumble upon action words like offered, moved, went, and waited. Faith isn't just something that we can say that we have; there'll be a testing of that faith, which requires some sort of demonstration.

If God has promised that He has our best interests at heart (Jeremiah 29:11) and has given us a glimpse of our destiny, yet current circumstances look nothing like that future place, do we sulk and complain or wait with confidence and joy on the Lord? If we're afflicted with an illness and we've been given a word of healing or have read the many stories of healing in the Bible, do we assume those stories aren't meant for our situation or do we act in faith that we'll be healed? If God has told us to move in a certain direction or tries to separate us from what we think is inseparable, do we trust Him and move or do we hang on to the old place or thing that He's moving us from?

The answers to these questions reveal if we really have the faith in Him that we claim to have. I know that I'm very guilty of "believing" in faith but not acting in faith. These two don't go together. Faith can only be demonstrated by an action. In any event, a demonstrable and outward expression of faith is the evidence of the inward truth. It begins with a mindset and heart condition and is later revealed by how we behave.

Let today be the day that you truly ask God to search your heart and reveal your true beliefs about Him. Are you relying on yourself or are you trusting in Him? There really isn't an in-between.

My Prayer

Lord God, thank You for Your faithfulness. You're merciful and loving. You provide for us over and over again. I pray, Lord, that the person reading this message will be moved to act in faith; that they will seek You out earnestly if they feel lost or unsure about the direction that You have for their life. I pray that their inward voice is silent so that they can hear Your still, small voice. And for those who are sure how You've been directing them, let them act in obedience. Give patience to those who are in a waiting period. Give diligence and perseverance to those who are being actively pruned and trained but are ready to give up. Give comfort to those who are afflicted. Lord, I know that this life won't always be comfortable; bad things will happen, unfortunately. Lord, please don't let us walk away from You or question Your love for us because of bad things that might happen. Silence those thoughts from the enemy and renew the hearts of those who have been wounded or hurt by others. Reassure them that faith in You isn't a waste of time. For those who don't know You, I pray for blessed assurance that they need You as their Lord and Savior. Touch their hearts right now, and let them have the faith to believe that You'll forgive them no matter what they've done. I thank You, Lord, for the power You possess and for the portion of that power that You're willing to extend to us if we just have faith in You. In Jesus's name I pray, Amen.

Day 21: Easing the Path for Our Children

The righteous man walks in his integrity; His
children are blessed after him.
Proverbs 20:7 (NKJV)

There are lots of parenting books out there with titles like "Being a Better Parent" or "Raising Happy Children." I'm not critiquing such books, and even though I've never invested in any of them, I've prayed a lot and wondered a lot and worried a lot about my children. I wonder if they'll grow up to really understand the power of God and prayer. And I wonder if they'll fall into the trap of sin set for them by the enemy. I also wonder if they'll finally go to God once they've experienced failure (like I did).

I worry about what type of example we are setting for our children. Are they going to mimic all the things that they see at home (which may not always be the best example)? Or will they follow what they see out there in the big wide world? So, yes, I'm concerned about the impact that I have on my children. This verse makes parenting quite simple—if we, as parents, live with integrity, then we leave the right type of legacy and heritage for our children. It's always good to keep in mind that children get to know their parents/guardians first before they ever get to know God. So if we can live with integrity, our children will get to know God in an entirely new way. Perhaps they can trust Him more immediately. Many people haven't had that chance growing up and can therefore wonder how "this God" they've never seen or touched could possibly love them more than their own earthly parents, who birthed them. This takes time to fully understand.

The point is if we pave the path for our children, not by beating them over the head with "what the Bible says" but by how we live our own lives, then we're able to show them that God can OF COURSE love them. Once you learn that God isn't just a bigger human, but rather righteous and perfect, then it may be easier to accept that He loves us. If an imperfect person can make an attempt to live a life of integrity, imagine what a perfect God can show you.

Now don't self-loathe because you haven't been the pillar of perfection for your children. That's not the expectation. Our first and most immediate step is to confess our sins to God. The next step is to open up more to our children (in an age-appropriate way) about what we ourselves struggle with. For example, if you get cut off by someone while driving and use a curse word, you can immediately say out loud, "Lord please forgive me for using bad language! Please forgive me for allowing my anger to get the best of me." Then say to your child, "I was wrong for using a bad word. I'm working on patience and using my mouth to bless others, not to curse them."

Living with integrity doesn't mean that we do no wrong. However, it does require us to live in constant prayer and confess IMMEDIATELY to God and those we've wronged. Integrity requires us to consistently live with transparency so that our kids can see not only when we do right, but also how we conduct ourselves when we do wrong.

My Prayer

Lord God, I sometimes struggle to live with integrity. It's a core value, but in my selfish ways, I sometimes fall into doing what I want and doing it the way I want it. That's not the example I want my children to see, nor do I want them to have a difficult walk because of negative seeds that I've planted in them. Lord, forgive me for not setting the right example for my children. Release me from any guilt I may feel. Instead, replace the guilt with a renewed sense of love for you. I pray that the reader of this message doesn't fall prey to the wiles of the enemy, who seeks to entrap us into guilt and self loathing over our parenting mistakes. I pray that You encourage our hearts and minds and show us the areas that You require change, so that we can be a blessing to our children. And I pray that You instill a spirit of forgiveness right now in those who've been wronged by their parents; that they'll not hold their parents hostage for inability or ignorance about this Scripture. Lord, we need You to be the people who You've called us to be. We thank You for Your Word. Thank You for loving us even when we're disobedient. We love You. In Jesus's name I pray, Amen.

Day 22: Shaking an Angry Fist

> Since prayer is at the bottom of all this, what I
> want mostly is for men to pray—not shaking
> angry fists at enemies but raising holy hands to
> God. And I want women to get in there with the
> men in humility before God, not primping before a
> mirror or chasing the latest fashions but doing
> something beautiful for God and becoming
> beautiful doing it.
> I Timothy 2:8-10 (MSG)

How do you handle it when someone disagrees with you? I tend to get angry, but I keep the anger inside. On the other hand, in closer, more intimate relationships, it can turn into an all-out brawl. We argue and fuss until one of us gets irritated enough to stop. In all of that, my approach is exactly what the verse says NOT to do—shaking an angry fist.

This verse isn't talking about our personal relationships, per se, but rather how we deal with our enemies or non-believers. However, the same premise must prevail. Humility and love have to be exercised. It takes humility to remember that "but God," or you might be in the same depraved state or dark place as the non-believer. Self-righteousness is never the proper posture.

Sometimes we get caught up in the belief that our former habitual sins (maybe even current ones—laziness, lying, etc.) aren't "as bad as" the sins of others. Those are all lies from the enemy. For we have ALL fallen short of the glory of God (Romans 3:9-10). Even the best human efforts are like filthy rags when compared to God's righteousness (Isaiah 64:6).

The point is that if we're to bring others to the saving grace of Christ, it will be through love. Our only responsibility is to share that same love and grace shown to us by Christ.

My Prayer

Lord, please forgive us for thinking ourselves better than we are. We're ONLY who and what we are because of the blood of Jesus—thank You. Please give us the love and grace we need to demonstrate to others so they may come to know You. Let us take the opportunity to speak boldly, but lovingly, to others about You. Prick our hearts when we allow our pride or fear to blind us of those opportunities. We love You and want to do Your will in the little things we do today. Help us to see Your deeds and be still long enough to praise You for it. In Jesus's name, Amen.

Day 23: Willingly Receive Him

> ...and they were afraid. But He said to them, "It is I; do not be afraid." Then they willingly received Him into the boat, and immediately the boat was at the land where they were going.
> John 6:19-21 (NKJV)

I'll begin this message with three words: **fear, willingness,** and **immediate**. What do these words have in common? In the midst of this powerful and dynamic chapter, there are verses that really jolt me when I'm taking the time to read carefully. Simply put, here is how this portion of the passage goes:

- The disciples were rowing the boat to get to Capernaum.
- Jesus was not in sight (it was dark).
- The disciples saw Jesus walking on water.
- They were afraid (OF COURSE!).
- He told them not to be fearful.
- They took him into the boat (WILLINGLY).
- He immediately took them to their destination.

What began as a fearful experience for the disciples ended in them getting to their destination IMMEDIATELY! Why does this stand out for me? I think of the many times that I'm feeling stuck and unproductive. I'm fighting to get to a new place in my spiritual walk, in my marriage, in my career, in my mind—the list goes on and on. But like the disciples, I'm rowing along in the dark trying to get there. Usually, at least for me, I eventually become frustrated, wondering why the heck it's taking so long to get to this new place! I generally grow fearful if the "winds begin to blow," meaning when trouble emerges or when the path gets murky. Sometimes I'm mature enough to inquire of God if I've missed His direction somewhere on the path. I almost always question if I made a wrong turn somewhere.

This passage has given me light to a new truth. Perhaps the issue is that I haven't WILLINGLY accepted Jesus into my boat. By "my boat," I mean my plan or vision. Has He been walking in the dark waters all along, waiting for me to invite Him in (willingly)? I think it's interesting that although Jesus could have stepped into the boat without the invitation from the disciples, this Scripture points out that they willingly took Him in. In fact, He didn't NEED to be on the boat at all! He could merely walk on the water. It was the disciples who needed Him on the boat. It was to their benefit. They no longer had to row because He immediately got them to their destination! Amazing!

Applying this Scripture to our lives would be to evaluate if we've somehow closed our minds, plans, and ideas off from Jesus. Have we willingly invited Him in? Or have we allowed fear to cripple us, even though He is saying, "Do not be afraid?" I believe that once we overcome our fears and trust Him by willingly inviting Him, He'll immediately take us to the "land where we're going."

My Prayer

Lord God, thank You for Your truth! Your power is so amazing to me that it simply leaves me in awe. When I release my expectations and fears and allow You into every crevice of my being, I know You'll move me immediately to the place You've destined me to be all along. I'm the barrier at times, and I ask You to forgive me for allowing my selfishness or disobedience to hinder the work You want to do in me. I know that part of being human and in this world is that storms will come; life won't be easy. But in the midst of the storms, I pray we're reminded that You're right there. Help us to see You when we allow ourselves to grow blind or deaf to You. Draw us back to You if we've wandered. I pray that the reader of this message will have fresh perspective about their current situation and renewed sense of courage and strength to continue to press on. I pray that You soften our hearts and create a willing spirit within us. Thank You, Lord, for Your faithfulness and love toward us. In Jesus's name I pray, Amen.

Day 24: Is it Love?

Love suffers long and is kind; love does not
envy; love does not parade itself, is not puffed
up; does not behave rudely, does not seek its
own, is not provoked, thinks no evil...
1 Corinthians 13:4-5 (NKJV)

Considering how rude I can be towards my loved ones, reading these verses makes me say, "Ouch!" My excuse is that they're rude to me. I don't think such an excuse will hold much water when I have to stand before the Lord. These verses shine a light on my poor behavior and remind me of how the Lord defines love. He defines it for us as never giving up, caring for others more than ourselves, being patient and so on.

Bottom line, love is an action. It's not just what you claim to "feel" on the inside. If you only feel it and the other person never experiences what you claim to feel, then it might be wise to go back and re-evaluate your love. Maybe you have a tendency to put yourself first or give up when things don't feel good. We can't change the way we are on our own. But we can take responsibility and confess it, then allow the Lord to change our heart's condition. We usually get stuck in our pride, and we don't admit that our ways are actually unlovable and not "okay" with the Lord.

My Prayer

Lord, I know that I frequently fail You in how I love others. I want to receive love, but I don't readily give it at times. I can be so rude sometimes, especially to the very person who I'm called to love the most intimately. I confess this nasty disposition and seek Your forgiveness. Lord, please give me a heart transplant. I want to love the way You've defined it, and I know I need You in order to do so. Please prick my heart when I'm not demonstrating love. We need You, Lord. I thank You for giving us the true definition and demonstration of Love when You sent Your one and only Son to the Cross; just for us. I love You, Lord. Thank You for Your wonderful, unconditional love. In Jesus's name I pray, Amen.

Day 25: Being Steadfast

Therefore, my beloved brethren, be steadfast, immovable, always abounding in the work of the Lord, knowing that your labor is not in vain in the Lord.
1 Corinthians 15:58 (NKJV)

This Scripture encourages us not to give up on the work assigned to us by the Lord. Sometimes it feels like our God-given work has no purpose or impact. I know that I personally struggle with this battle, especially in the world of social justice work that I do. It tends to feel like positive change isn't happening, that no amount of change is enough. This can be downright frustrating. I do believe that the Lord wants me to do this work, but at times, I'm not steadfast or immovable. I want to give up, and I start doing something different. At a few junctures, I've actually quit out of frustration.

Even if your work is in another discipline and you know it's the Lord's desire for you to do that work, don't give up. The results that you seek may not necessarily be what God desires, but don't assume that your work is in vain just because the impact you want isn't obvious. Be steadfast as the Scripture says! This may apply to your marriage, job, ministry, or your parenting "work" with your children. Be immovable, and praise God for the encouragement to keep doing what He has instructed you to do.

My Prayer

Lord, we thank You for encouraging us with Your Word. We frequently use our emotions instead of Your Word; please forgive us. Make us immovable and steadfast where we've become weary. Show us Your perspective, and blind us to our own if it doesn't align with Your will for our lives. Renew our minds and energize our hearts. If we've lost our path, please set us straight so that we may get busy doing Your work. Thank You, Lord, for another chance. In Jesus's name I pray, Amen.

Day 26: Stop Freaking Out

Which of you by worrying can add one cubit to
his stature?
Matthew 6:27 (NKJV)

Do you remember a moment when you found yourself freaking out? At one point in my life, the "freak-out mode" was a constant reality. In fact, I'm not sure that I had any other mode, sadly. I was always trying to attain perfection in everything I did. What I've learned is that the need for things to be perfect is exhausting and leads to one freak-out after another. For me, things have always felt out of control or simply out of balance. The reality was that "things" were just doing what they do. I was the one reacting with panic to various responsibilities and too many things on the calendar.

Even though I'm "cured" of this exhausting way of being, old habits still creep in periodically. But now I can at least stop and take a moment to quiet the craziness in my mind. I ask myself how big of a deal whatever I'm freaking out about really is in the grand scheme of things. During my last attack of the worries, I asked the Lord for a Word to stop the uneasiness and worry. This Scripture popped up in my mind and reminded me not to allow human reasoning to take over, but to live by faith in what the Lord has said through His Word. My worry produces nothing, and while I already know that, I still need a reminder every once in a while. I know that I have God's protection. But it's not because I'm doing things perfectly, for sure. It's because of Him; because of Jesus.

My Prayer

Thank You, Lord, for Your Word! When I begged You for a Word to motivate me and set my steps right, I expected harshness. But instead, I was given a kind hug by Your Word; how timely. Lord, allow the reader of this message to be moved to release the spirit of anxiety and allow You to truly guide them. I ask for forgiveness for my wayward attitude and behavior. Please guide us, Lord, and give us that fresh desire to seek after You, no matter what. Thank You for loving us, for saving us, and for Your favor and grace, in Jesus's name, Amen.

Day 27: Empowered by His Presence

Call to Me, and I will answer you, and show you
great and mighty things, which you do not know.
Jeremiah 33:3 (NKJV)

I believe that people feel empowered for a variety of reasons. For me, I tend to feel empowered when I'm given the freedom and trust to act on a good idea or when I'm not micromanaged. At home, empowerment is a bit different. I feel empowered when I have the affirmation of my family. But none of these examples are rooted in the type of empowerment that the Lord intends for us. This Scripture reminds us that all the Lord wants us to do is to call on Him. There's so much about our lives, our paths, and our future that we don't know. No matter how smart we claim to be, He knows so much more than we ever will.

I'm reminded by this Scripture that the Lord's presence is greatly empowering. Once He steps into a situation, it changes. The circumstances may not change, but He'll produce change in our hearts, which ultimately changes the way that we approach the situation. The Lord removes the scales from our eyes. He sensitizes us to hear Him softly, encouraging or directing us. All we have to do is follow one simple principle—call to Him.

I tend to wait until I'm in a mess before I cry for help! But the maturing Christian woman in me strives to seek the Lord at all times, be specific with my request, and earnestly listen for His answer. This verse says, "I WILL answer," not I MIGHT answer. If we call, He'll answer. His mighty presence will empower us to do the great and mighty things that He has in store for us to support His kingdom here on earth. If you're feeling lost, unenthused, or downright hopeless, look up—call to Him, and be prepared for His presence to empower you in a new way.

My Prayer

Lord, thank You for Your promises. At times, we waver in our faith, especially when things aren't going as we planned. Please remind us that You indeed **will** *answer us; that You'll show us great and mighty things. May the reader of this message feel a heart change right now just in knowing that You'll answer. I pray for hope for those who are feeling hopeless and increased faith for those who've been wavering. Bless us with Your presence. Empower us with Your strength. Thank You for Your love and Your tender mercies. In Jesus's name I pray, Amen.*

Day 28: Worrying Produces Nothing!

> Look at the birds of the air, for they neither sow
> nor reap nor gather into barns; yet your heavenly
> Father feeds them. Are you not of more value
> than they?
> Matthew 6:26 (NKJV)

As I mentioned a few days ago, unfortunately, I've been guilty of playing a defeating game with my mind and spirit. During a long season of my life, worry entrapped me so much that I would panic and worry if I wasn't worried about something! Literally, I would begin to search the recesses of my mind, asking myself, "What should I be worried about today?" What an awful way to live. Worry robs us of joy and peace and, more importantly, it puts us in a position that's against the faith walk God has for us.

Don't get me wrong, I still retreat back into worrywart zone from time to time, and even while I worried, I prayed. Those closest to me would always ask, "Why pray if you're going to worry anyway?" The saving grace for me is that I finally came to the reality, through a lot of meditating on this Scripture and much prayer, that worry produces nothing. Absolutely nothing! In fact, all that worry does is to produce more worry.

The problem with worry is that it puts us into a mental space where we lose our ability to be grateful, consequently leading to a loss of joy. One of my favorite authors, Brene Brown, calls this joy-stealing worry "squandering joy." Over time, we become really good at finding ways to "rain on the parade" and seeing the negative in situations rather than nurturing a grateful spirit, which actually breeds more ungratefulness.

If you struggle with the ailment of worry, read this Scripture and Matthew 6:34 repeatedly. Each time worry seeps into your spirit, read and recite those Scriptures. Keep in the front of your mind that God truly has your best interest at heart. You have to believe that He sees you as more valuable than anything. Once you've done that, then accept the gift of love and peace that Jesus has given you. If things in your life are spinning out of control and you're feeling crazy, take a moment to pray and thank God for all the things that have gone well.

Let today be the day that you stop the worry cycle. You too can have joy, and all it takes is a deliberate practice of thankfulness and looking for reasons to be grateful instead of reasons to worry. I promise you that you'll find yourself in a more peaceful place if you try this out repeatedly.

My Prayer

Lord God, please forgive us for not following Your Word. You remind us in so many ways through Your Word that worry has no place in a faithful heart. I ask You to remove the spirit of worry from anyone suffering from such a heavy spirit. Please remind us that Your loving spirit is light and easy, not heavy and burdensome. The enemy seeks to kill our spirits, steal our light, and destroy our joy. I pray that we see the spirit of worry as a dagger from the enemy instead of falling prey to his tactics. Help us use the armor that You've given us, seeking You in prayer and confessing that we've chosen worry over faith in You. Thank you, Lord, for forgiving us, and I celebrate in advance the burdens that'll be lifted by the end of this prayer. For those who are burdened by heavy pains, grief, loss of employment, or other traumatic events, I pray that You give them peace and comfort right now and remove the worry from their hearts. Thank You, Lord, for loving us so much and for having our best interests at heart. In Jesus's name, I pray and give You thanks. Amen.

> But what happens when we live God's way? He brings gifts into our lives, much the same way that fruit appears in an orchard—things like affection for others, exuberance about life, serenity. We develop a willingness to stick with things, a sense of compassion in the heart, and a conviction that a basic holiness permeates things and people.
> Galatians 5:22-23 (MSG)

This Scripture speaks for itself; no devotion needed for today! Each time I read this Scripture, I sigh, nod, and then think, "CRAP! I'm not living God's way!" I think of how I struggle to fight against my flesh; how desperately I want things my way (of course, my way is the right way!) This Scripture is truly convicting and, at the same time, very reassuring. It reminds me if I choose to do it His way, then the things that I ultimately have been trying to get all along will be mine. I'm not referring to "things" such as possessions, but I mean character traits.

I often struggle to commit to hard tasks; I tend to want to give up easily. Yet in my heart, I want to do the things referenced in Galatians 5:22-23. I want to be able to commit. I also want serenity; I want to be affectionate toward others. And I want to be energized about life. In order for me to acquire all of these, what I have to do is simply put aside my own selfish desires and allow the things that are getting in my way to be crucified.

Perhaps the struggle is really that God tries to crucify this selfish, prideful spirit within me, but I won't allow Him. If I release it and truly allow Him to be the center of my life, then I can become who I've been striving to be all along. It sounds easy, but it takes a bit of discipline and a choice to truly do it His way, not mine!

My Prayer

Lord, thank You for Your Word, which is our light and gives us the direction we need to live this life. Please forgive us for our selfish ways and for choosing to do things according to our own will. We want to live according to Your way; please give us the desire to do so. Give us the discipline, Lord, to say no to anything that gets in our way of living by Your Word, even if we're the problem. Do whatever it takes to remove the barriers, and open our minds and hearts to receive the gift of life that You've given us. For those who don't know You as their personal Lord and Savior, please bring them to You so that they too can enjoy the free gift of salvation that You died for on our behalf. Thank You, Lord, for Your love and mercy. In Jesus's name I pray and give You thanks. Amen.

Day 30: Utterly Incapable

Out of sheer generosity, he put us in right
standing with himself. A pure gift. He got us out
of the mess we're in and restored us to where he
always wanted us to be. And he did it by means
of Jesus Christ.
Romans 3:24 (MSG)

Yesterday, I discussed the easy task of living God's way (and by easy, I'm being extremely sarcastic). There may be some among you who find it easy to live a Godly life. But I'll honestly tell you that I don't find it easy at all! I'm selfish and prideful, and even in my best efforts, I still fall short of God's glory. This Scripture provides me with perspective on how I'm to live God's way in spite of my shortcomings.

God knows that we're utterly incapable of doing the things that we need to do to be in right standing with Him. That doesn't mean that He is sitting on His throne saying, "Yep, keep being a heathen! Live however you want to!" No, just the opposite. To help folks like me, He felt so much love (and probably pity for my simple self) and restored me through Jesus Christ, allowing me to be in right standing with Him. He loves us so much that He puts aside our mess so that we can have what He has in store for each of us.

In fact, this Scripture makes me think of my own children. Suppose I have a priceless gift for them, how would I proceed if they are unloving, rude, deceitful, and liars? Would I go through all sorts of things to find a way to give them this priceless gift? Heavy sigh—no, probably not. But literally, that's what God does. He wants us to have his grace and love so much, knowing it brings peace, that he has justified us (all of our past, present, and future sins) through His only Son, Jesus Christ. It's quite amazing and extremely humbling to conceive that God loves us so much. With this knowledge, it means that I can at least make a small effort to be better today than I was yesterday.

How can we show God today that we're grateful for the priceless gift He has given us (which we don't deserve)? Maybe by giving to the poor, forgiving someone, or simply saying, "Thank You, Lord!"

My Prayer

Lord, thank You so much for doing what I'm incapable of achieving on my own. You know, in Your endless wisdom, what my shortcomings are and that I want to be in right standing with You; yet I struggle. Knowing all I have done, my thoughts, and even knowing what I'll do in the future, You still allowed me to be saved through Your Son, Jesus Christ. I thank You for loving me in such an individual way. No one on this earth could possibly display that type of love. I pray that the reader struggling to feel Your love receives a kind word or gesture today that demonstrates a small sliver of Your love. And if anyone reading this struggles to believe and accept You, please give them the saving grace to recognize that You're there— waiting with open arms to accept them in the same way that You've accepted me. Thank You, Lord. I pray in Your Son's loving name, Jesus Christ. Amen!

Day 31: How Much Mercy Do We Get?

> For as the heavens are high above the earth, So great is His mercy toward those who fear Him; As far as the east is from the west, So far has He removed our transgressions from us.
> Psalms 103:11-12 (NKJV)

Sitting among God's creations really makes me appreciate just how high the heavens are from earth and just how far the east is from the west. Listening to the deep roar of the waves as they rise up then gently roll onto the beach also reminds me of the power and gentleness of God. How amazing! It's hard to understand how God could be so awesome.

Reading this Scripture takes the thought of how awesome God is to a higher level of gratitude. This Scripture reminds us that His mercy and forgiveness are truly expansive. The visual before me (of an unobstructed view of the sky and earth) really intensifies and consecrates this truth. If you're feeling like you've done something that God can't forgive you for, you're wrong. If you feel like your situation is so bad that He can't fix it, you're wrong. All you need to do is believe in Him with a faithful heart, and confess your sins. He'll show mercy (endlessly) towards you.

A word of caution—experiencing God's mercy doesn't mean your problems will go away. In fact, they could intensify. But your perspective and heart will change. You'll go from an attitude of complaining and worrying to one of gratefulness. Suddenly, things won't seem so bad, or at least you'll feel more hopeful. This hopeful feeling provides a burst of clarity, like the rays of the sun breaching the horizon at dawn. You'll suddenly realize that the insurmountable problems you're faced with are actually conquerable.

Try confessing your worst sin today. Be specific; God already knows about it anyway, so you can't really fool Him. Try believing Him to fix you from the inside out. God's mercy is expansive.

My Prayer

Lord, thank You for having mercy on us. We don't deserve it, but You give it to us time and time again. You show us Your love; You forgive us, then we mess up again. But You're so faithful to forgive us again. Thank You! Please heal any brokenness that keeps us from truly trusting You. If someone reading this doesn't know You, please open their heart to receive You. Forgive them, and make them whole again. Thank You for Your love and for the blood of Jesus that covers us. It's in His name that I pray and give You thanks. Amen.

Note Pages

Use these pages to scribble your favorite
Scriptures or reflections as you take this 31-day
journey.